Also by Dave Malone

Fiction
Purgatory: A Good Way to Die (Butterworth)
Not Forgiven, Not Forgotten

Poetry
View from the North Ten: Poems after
Mark Rothko's No. 15
Seasons in Love
Under the Sycamore
23 Sonnets
Poems to Love & the Body

THE HEARTS
OF
BLUE WHALES

THE HEARTS
OF
BLUE WHALES

a play

Dave Malone and Kerry Doan

Trask Road Press   West Plains, MO   2014

The Hearts of Blue Whales debuted at the Avenue Theatre in West Plains, Missouri, on June 1, 2012. The play ran during the 2012 transit of Venus.

Dave Malone directed the play. The cast included Candi Williams as Jessie and Dustin Collins as Chance. Jenni Wichern created the set design.

The Hearts of Blue Whales was originally a screenplay written by Kerry McIntosh Doan and Dave Malone. On the weekend of September 16, 2005, Kerry and Dave met at his family's inn, Malone's Motel, in Mountain View, Missouri. They worked hard, imbibed a few beers, and finished a strong draft of the screenplay, which they later adapted into this stageplay.

for Jenni and Larry

THE HEARTS
OF
BLUE WHALES

CHARACTERS

CHANCE, in his late twenties, is a guitar player and a somewhat geeky guy, but he has rough and tumble good looks.

JESSIE is a no-nonsense gal in her late twenties.

These characters are from the Missouri Ozarks, so they will have a slight Ozark accent. Note: this accent is not a Southern drawl, but more Midwestern, with a certain cadence. For example, sometimes the letter Gs are dropped in ING words. For instance, "something" often becomes "somethin'."

SETTING
Kansas City. Hotel room and parking lot.

TIME
Early summer. Present day.

PRODUCTION NOTES
For the West Plains' production, the presumed bathroom was upstage right. The mirror and the beach scene art were on a stage right wall. The art #2 was on the stage left wall.

DIRECTOR'S CHOICE: ONE OR TWO ACTS
This play works as either a one-act or two-act performance. For ease of reading, the play is structured as a two-act play.

ACT ONE
SCENE ONE

Lights up on a clean, white room in a budget motel, like a Super 8. The room will have some art on the walls (one print should be a beach scene with sand dunes).

A room card, one of those brown ice buckets, coasters, coffee stirrers, coffee cups, and plastic cups rest on a small table. Two chairs flank the table. On the bed rests a small duffle bag.

CHANCE enters (from a presumed bathroom offstage). Dressed in blue jeans, he finishes snapping up a shirt that passes for pretty nice for a musician (a plaid Western shirt with pearl buttons would work). Chance surveys the room, as if to check its tidiness. But first, he checks himself in a full-length mirror. Then, he grabs a shirt off the bed and puts it in the duffle bag, then removes the bag from the bed and tucks it on the floor. He begins to straighten items on the table.

A knock at the door.

Chance doesn't like the way the duffle bag looks. Maybe he closes it tighter, maybe kicks it gently into submission.

He walks to the door and peeks through the peephole.

He opens the door. JESSIE walks in. She wears a sundress and carries a canvas tote.

JESSIE

Hi.

CHANCE

Hey.

*Both are not sure what to do, and they decide a
quick embrace is fine.*

CHANCE (CONT'D)

I appreciate ya coming by to pick me up, I—

JESSIE

It's no problem.

CHANCE

You know with the band. We've got the van and the trailer. I
don't have my car with me.

JESSIE

I understand. I'm just glad I was free for the evening.

CHANCE

Great.

*Chance motions her into the body of the room.
They remain standing.*

JESSIE

So you guys don't play tonight?

CHANCE

The other band got stuck in Vermont.

JESSIE

Really?

CHANCE

Delaware.

                    JESSIE
That's quite a ways—

                    CHANCE
No, the real skinny one.

                    JESSIE
Rhode Island?

                    CHANCE
Rhode Island.

                    JESSIE
Because there's a huge craze for foot-stompin' rock in New
England?

                    CHANCE
Those Yankees know how to foot stomp.

                    JESSIE
And you guys won't practice tonight?

          Chance gives her a certain look.

                JESSIE (CONT'D)
Of course not, you guys are pros.
          (Beat)
You got something to drink.

                    CHANCE
          (implying alcohol)
You're doing okay with it?

                    JESSIE
You got something to drink?

                    CHANCE
Just the thing.

*Chance goes to his duffle bag and pulls a fifth of
bourbon out of it.*

CHANCE (CONT'D)
I got this as a gift when we played Lexington. Limited edition
of Four Roses. Yeah?

JESSIE
Perfect.

*Jessie moves to the table and puts her tote on one
of the chairs. Chance makes it clear he will serve
her in a plastic cup.*

CHANCE
This is gonna be real classy.

*Jessie crosses to look at art (the beach scene
painting) on the wall. Chance starts to pour two
drinks.*

CHANCE (CONT'D)
I kinda like it.

JESSIE
Sand dunes?

CHANCE
Sure. And the light, the tall grass.

JESSIE
It's kinda tough to think about the beach when you're locked
in Kansas City.

CHANCE
Does Mexican still sound good to you?

                            JESSIE
I was actually thinking Thai.

                            CHANCE
I could do Thai. That place on 39th?

                            JESSIE
Yeah.

              Chance crosses to Jessie and hands her the drink
              then raises his glass in toast.

                            CHANCE
Cheers.

              The bourbon is strong. It shows as they take a
              drink.

                       CHANCE (CONT'D)
A smidge better than my grandaddy's hooch, huh?

                            JESSIE
Nothing wrong with his white lightnin'.

              During the following speech, Jessie is
              uncomfortable and crosses to the table but does
              not sit down.

                            CHANCE
I almost forgot. That one time, it was hot as hell, we went
over there in my truck. Papa Hank gave it to us in those little
shot glasses he got from Florida, the ones with the smiling
alligator on 'em. And you had so much, you passed out in
the—

                            JESSIE
Is it just me or are motel rooms getting smaller?

CHANCE
Oh yeah. And the people bigger.

Chance slowly crosses to the table.

JESSIE
Kinda ironic.
    (Beat)
So.

Chance sits down, and Jessie follows suit, but removes her tote first and places it in the floor.

CHANCE
So.

JESSIE
Why did you call me after all this time? I mean, I'm glad you did. But I was just curious. I'm sure you guys have played Kansas City more than once over the last six years.

CHANCE
Yeah.
    (Beat)
You're gonna make fun.

JESSIE
I won't.

CHANCE
You will.

JESSIE
I might.

CHANCE
Can I make something up?

                    JESSIE

No.

                    CHANCE

A few falsehoods?

                    JESSIE

No.

                    CHANCE

All right. I called—

                    JESSIE

Are you going to get your cows over their buckets or what?

                    CHANCE

You still say that?

                    JESSIE

I still say that.

                    CHANCE

You can take the girl out of the Ozarks, but you can't take the
Ozarks out of the girl.

          Jessie has a visibly unpleasant reaction.

                    JESSIE

You're the one who started up with the cows and the
buckets.

                    CHANCE

I gave you that?

                    JESSIE

You gave me a lot of things.

CHANCE
You gave me a lot of things, too.

JESSIE
I guess that's what people do when they're romantically involved for days on end.

CHANCE
Was it days on end?

JESSIE
Figure of speech.

CHANCE
But days on end makes it sound—

JESSIE
Trite?

CHANCE
(less than annoyed)
Don't finish my sentences. It makes it sound
(Beat)
monotonous.

JESSIE
I didn't mean it that way.

CHANCE
We weren't monotonous.

JESSIE
I don't think we could have been accused of monotonous. A lot of other crazy shit but not monotonous. Are you going to answer my question?

CHANCE
What was the question?

                         JESSIE
                       (not angry)
              Why did you call me, ya'asshole?

                         CHANCE
              When was the last time we talked?

                         JESSIE
Like six years ago?

                         CHANCE
That's a long time.

                         JESSIE
Mm-hm.

                         CHANCE
I just wanted to know how you were.

                         JESSIE
That's it?

                         CHANCE
It's real simple, Jess. I just wanted to talk to you.

                         JESSIE
That's all?

                         CHANCE
                  (just a slight bit touchy)
Yeah.

                         JESSIE
Really?

            A tinge annoyed, Chance crosses slowly toward the
            bed.

CHANCE
(testy)
Yeah.

Chance sinks into the bed. He sits on its edge.

JESSIE
Are you mad at me for asking?

Awkward silence.

JESSIE (CONT'D)
This bourbon is good.

CHANCE
(distant)
It has hints of dark chocolate, roasted nuts, and honeysuckle.

JESSIE
Right.

CHANCE
(distant)
Says so on the bottle. It's a limited edition, single barrel.

JESSIE
It's very nice. You remember Dawn Holden, don't you? She lives in Louisville now and insists I come out every spring for Derby and drink mint juleps. But I don't.

CHANCE
(distant)
You should go. They party for like a week and a half.

JESSIE
I'd have to buy clothes.

                    CHANCE
You would?

                    JESSIE
Yes.

          Jessie crosses and sits on the edge of the bed next
          to Chance.

          As Jessie talks below, Chance's attitude shifts from
          his friendly intentions to something else. Chance
          becomes a bit enamored with Jessie and begins to
          think that they could have a future together.

                JESSIE (CONT'D)
They expect you to look a certain way, you know. Dawn sent
me a picture last year of her with Adrien Brody. Can you
imagine? And she was wearing this giant floppy hat. I'd have
to buy giant floppy hats.

                    CHANCE
But you don't like giant floppy hats.

                    JESSIE
And I don't like mint juleps.

                    CHANCE
They ruin it with the—

                    JESSIE
Yeah, they just really ruin it with the mint leaves.

                    CHANCE
Yep. They do a real number on it.

          Chance looks at Jessie in a way that betrays this
          new feeling he is having towards her.

                                                        15

Jessie calls his bluff by looking at him a certain way, and he erases or softens his look.

CHANCE (CONT'D)
You never did make much of a Southerner.

JESSIE
You do.

CHANCE
I don't.

JESSIE
You do.

CHANCE
I make a good Ozarker, not a Southerner.

JESSIE
There's a difference?

CHANCE
An Ozarker is an Ozarker. You know that.

JESSIE
Yeah, right. Like how Texas is a state?

CHANCE
Texas is a state.

JESSIE
Don't tell them that.
(Beat)
I've missed your sense of humor.

CHANCE
I've missed someone who could keep up with me.

JESSIE

Roadies and girl groupies not quick enough for you?

CHANCE

I've had deeper conversations with my beta fish.

JESSIE

You still have Franklin?

CHANCE

No, he passed away. I held a small service. You were in his last thoughts.

JESSIE

Remember my black lab, Othello?

CHANCE

Sure.

JESSIE

He's gone, too.

CHANCE

Another?

JESSIE

Desdemona.

CHANCE

Why do people insist on naming their pets after fictional characters? I can't believe you're in on it, too.

JESSIE

At least mine was in the same fuckin' play. For some of us pet owners, our animals are surrogate kids. And it's our way of being creative without harming the animal.

CHANCE

Except in name.

JESSIE

Sometimes the names are perfect. Didn't Franklin fit the spirit
of your beta fish? I thought Franklin was the perfect name.
You know, he was sort of a—

CHANCE

I heard the song.

JESSIE

What?

CHANCE

I heard the song. That's why I called.

JESSIE

What song?

CHANCE

Remember when we camped in the forest up past Willow?
When we were drivin' up, a song came on the radio. It was a
cover of that old David Bowie song, "Let's Dance." But it was
slowed way down. I heard it a few nights ago. It made me
think about you, so I wanted to call.

JESSIE

Well. I'm glad you did.

CHANCE

Do you remember the song?

JESSIE

No.
        (Beat)
But I remember that trip.

CHANCE
But it was like a lifetime ago for you?

JESSIE
Why do you say that?

CHANCE
Pretty easy to see you've tried to drive everything Ozark out
of you.
    (Beat)
But you and I know it ain't possible.

JESSIE
Yeah, well, that's all in the past.

CHANCE
Then why do I see all of it in your face right now?

        *Jessie rises from the bed, takes a drink, and crosses
        to the art on the wall closest to the table (opposite
        wall to the art earlier).*

JESSIE
Don't make this hard on me, Chance.

CHANCE
I don't want to. I just hate to see you like this. You know your
dad lost himself. You had nothing to do with it.

JESSIE
I was a burden to him. I always—

CHANCE
A child is not a burden unless the parent makes it so. Your
mom going back home to Oregon had nothing to do with you
either. It had to do with him.
    (Beat)
You saw him recently?

JESSIE

Last month.

CHANCE

Why?

JESSIE

You know why.

CHANCE

His usual stuff?

JESSIE

He'd been in a knife fight. He needed me.

CHANCE

And how much money did he steal out of your purse?

JESSIE

You don't know what it's like. You have two well-adjusted
parents who are still married.

CHANCE

You don't think everyone pays a price for that? They're not
happy. They're fuckin' roommates.

JESSIE

Yeah, well, at least they're not in jail or in the hospital.

CHANCE

Pick your poison.

Jessie downs her drink.

JESSIE

This bourbon is tasty. Let's have another.

CHANCE

You got this?

JESSIE

You can make it a small one if you're so worried about me.

CHANCE

I'm just a lightweight. I'm going to need fuel pretty soon.

JESSIE
(strong, but poking fun)

Baby.

CHANCE
(exhaling, unable to retort)

I got nothin.'

Chance crosses to the table and begins to pour her another small drink and tops his to match.

CHANCE (CONT'D)

You look good. KC treatin' you all right?

JESSIE

Thanks. Yeah, I have a good job working as a paralegal for a new law firm.

Chance hands her a drink.

JESSIE (CONT'D)

Thank you.

Jessie sits down at the table, and Chance does, too.

JESSIE (CONT'D)

They know I'm into acting, so they let me go for auditions. I've got a small role in the next Shakespeare play at the Rep.

CHANCE

That's fantastic.

JESSIE

But I've got a lead role in a new play with a small theater. Written by a local girl. Kind of *Sex and the City* meets Tom Clancy thriller.

CHANCE

That's awesome.

JESSIE

I can't help but notice the band is doing well.

CHANCE

The label is good to us.

JESSIE

And you're good to the label.

CHANCE

Yeah, well. I'm just going with it.

JESSIE

You're not far from a huge concert tour.

CHANCE

Bigger tour, bigger problems. I guess that's what you deal with all day, other people's problems, right? The life of a paralegal?

JESSIE

Yeah. Last week, a guy came in who lost his sixteen-year old daughter who got in a car crash.

CHANCE

Ah jees.

JESSIE

She had this gorgeous curly hair, a great smile, and all these
hopes and dreams. The dad wanted to blame the highway
department for a sign that wasn't there. But the truth is, his
daughter was driving way too fast.

CHANCE

That's terrible.

JESSIE

She was here a week ago. Sixteen, full of life, now she's gone.
She's just a period. Her sentence has been written. I think
about that. One day, and you never know when, my sentence
is going to be written.

Chance looks at her a certain, fond way.

CHANCE

I remember the first time—

JESSIE

All right, let's not get into any nostalgic crap, or I'll tear up or
something.

CHANCE

Ya know, a few minutes ago, I realized, this is good what's
happening here.

JESSIE

What's happening here?

CHANCE

This.

JESSIE

What this?

CHANCE

You and me interacting.

JESSIE

It's what human beings do.

CHANCE

And it's what human beings do who connect with each other.

JESSIE

Which I suppose is why we did what we did six years ago.

CHANCE

Did you ever feel like we gave up too early?

JESSIE

Is this what this is about?

CHANCE

What *what* is about?

JESSIE

The phone call, the dinner? I thought it was just you, hearing a song, then calling me—wait. No, what I really thought before I got here was that your band was playing, an opening band cancelled because they're stuck in a monsoon in New Hampshire—

CHANCE

Rhode Island.

JESSIE

Whatever, and that you had an extra night, so you called me.

CHANCE

That is what this is. I heard the song. I thought it might be nice to talk to you again, so I called. That's—

JESSIE

It doesn't sound like that.

CHANCE

What does it sound like?

JESSIE

Don't make me say it. You did have something more than a
fourth grade education.

CHANCE

Actually, I finished my bachelor's while you were mourning
Othello and I was mourning Franklin.
(Beat)
What? Do you think I planned this out? That I had some kind of
scheme to woo you with the finest bourbon on the planet,
and then go to one of the best Mexican dives in the city, and
then what? That I had some devious plan to get us back
together? Jesus.

JESSIE

I'm just sayin' what it looks like from here.

CHANCE

Well, open your eyes. I might be clever, but I'm not conniving.

JESSIE

This is nice. We're just a few minutes away from yelling at
each other at the top of our lungs. I can see how things
between us would work out just peachy.

CHANCE

As if healthy discussion isn't part of how two people work
things out.

JESSIE

What are you talking about? We're not two people working
things out. We're strangers.

CHANCE

I don't believe that. Weren't you here for the last ten minutes? We're easy with each other.

> *Astounded by this, Jessie rises and crosses and walks toward the art. She can move a bit but end up center stage.*

JESSIE

When things aren't difficult. When things don't have an agenda.

CHANCE

I don't have a bloody agenda.

JESSIE

It feels like you have an agenda.

CHANCE

I don't. The only thing I can figure is that when I mentioned I was feeling a feeling of connection here, you went nuts, and got all defensive about it, then spun your own twist on it.

JESSIE

Twists or no twists, it felt like an agenda.

CHANCE

It wasn't.
    (Beat)
And nuts was an inappropriate word.

JESSIE

Thank you.

> *Chance rises and crosses to center stage near Jessie.*

CHANCE

This just feels really good. Why not go with it?

JESSIE

I'm not single.

Long pause.

CHANCE

I'm sure the food's gonna be great.

JESSIE

I haven't had Mexican in a while.

CHANCE

Thai.

JESSIE

Right.

Chance goes to the table and gets his room card. Jessie downs her drink.

Jessie grabs her tote and then begins to exit first. Chance follows, and they exit.

Lights down.

ACT ONE
SCENE TWO

Lights up.

Chance and Jessie enter the motel room.

While Jessie talks below, she'll throw her tote beneath the table.

Chance crosses toward the mirror to inspect himself—and his teeth (only when Jessie is not watching, of course).

JESSIE
No, the best part was the time we took Isaiah to that Japanese restaurant, and he doused his dinner with wasabi. And then before he got finished, his nose was bleeding because it was so fuckin' hot.

CHANCE
No, the best part was that they kicked him out of the restaurant.

JESSIE
Oh, he was ready to leave by that point anyway.

CHANCE
When he was still wearing his napkin like a bib?

Jessie grabs the bottle of bourbon.

JESSIE

May I?

CHANCE

Aren't you good?

                    JESSIE
I had one glass of wine, and only one glass of wine, at dinner.
                    (Beat)
Want one?

                    CHANCE
No, I'm okay.

          Jessie begins her pour.

                    JESSIE
This was quite a gift. You didn't say who gave it to you.

                    CHANCE
Club owner.

                    JESSIE
What was she like?

                    CHANCE
He.

          *With drink in hand, Jessie kicks off her shoes and
          plops onto the middle of the bed. She props a
          pillow behind her back and leans against the
          headboard. Chance crosses toward the table.*

                CHANCE (CONT'D)
He was generous.

          *Chance sits in the chair closest to the bed and
          positions it so they can talk. Jessie takes a sip of
          her drink.*

                    JESSIE
This is the only reason I'm in your room.

CHANCE
I believe that's what you believe.

JESSIE
(a touch testy)
What's that supposed to mean, Obi-Wan?

CHANCE
Nothing. I just like to see that temper start to flare.

JESSIE
Am I that easy to get worked up?

CHANCE
Something like that.

JESSIE
I got it from my red-headed father. Blame him.
(Beat)
Hold me to one bourbon. Promise? I have to work tomorrow.

CHANCE
On a Saturday?

JESSIE
Especially on a Saturday.
(Beat)
Thanks for indulging me on the Thai.

CHANCE
It's one of my favorites, too.

> *A seriously loud knock on the door. Chance goes to
> the door, looks through the peephole, and opens
> the door enough to be conversational.*

                    VOICE OFF STAGE
            (loudly)
Dude!

                        CHANCE
What's up, man?

                    VOICE OFF STAGE
            (loudly)
Dude! We're parytin' in 204!

                        CHANCE
I'm right here.

            At first uninterested, then Jessie moves in the bed,
            so she can eavesdrop on the conversation. We only
            hear Chance's responses.

                    CHANCE (CONT'D)
I'm not going to put in an appearance...You guys don't need
me...you don't...get out of here...go...don't look at me like
that.

                    VOICE OFF STAGE
Dude!

            Chance closes the door. Chance crosses and sits
            back down at the table in the chair closest to the
            bed and Jessie.

                        JESSIE
You should go.

                        CHANCE
Ah, so you can translate "Drunk"?

                        JESSIE
It's a language I've studied up on pretty well. You should go.

CHANCE

I shouldn't go.

JESSIE

Didn't you just tell "Dude" you'd make an appearance?

CHANCE

Is that what I said?

JESSIE

You don't plan to make an appearance and see April?

CHANCE

I was wrong. You are a scholar of the Drunk language. April's the manager for the record label. I won't be missed. Isaiah can suck up for us.

JESSIE

If I weren't here, would you go?

CHANCE

But you are here.

JESSIE

And if I weren't?

CHANCE

I'm not good at hypotheticals, Jess.

JESSIE

Why not?

CHANCE

It's either happening or it isn't. What about you?

JESSIE

What about me what?

CHANCE
If you weren't here, then—

JESSIE
What would I be doing?

CHANCE
Mm-hm.

JESSIE
(deep in thought)
Probably talking to my plants.

CHANCE
(gently poking fun)
It's truly a miracle you're here with me right now.

JESSIE
No, it's they just look really bad. And they say you're
supposed to talk to your plants, right?

CHANCE
That's what they say.

JESSIE
My hibiscus looks terrible.

CHANCE
Aren't they pretty hardy?

JESSIE
Exactly.

CHANCE
Sounds like a fun evening.

JESSIE

Oh, I'm sure Susan would pester me and—do you remember
Susan?

Chance nods.

JESSIE (CON'TD)

She'd convince me to go out for beers. We'd talk about her
dreadful love life and her great aunt who wears prom dresses,
smokes cigarettes and bake cookies as if it was still 1955.

CHANCE

And if Susan doesn't call you?

JESSIE

Oh. Probably snuggled up in bed with Desdemona and this
book on Amelia Earhart. Do you know that her body was
never recovered? Of course, they didn't discover Ambrose
Bierce's body either?

CHANCE

The short story writer?

JESSIE

Yeah. "Occurrence at Owl Creek Bridge." Remember?

CHANCE

Oh yeah. The one everyone—

JESSIE

Everyone had—

JESSIE (CONT'D)

Had to read in high school.
    (*Beat*)
I'm sorry I interrupted you.

CHANCE

No, that's okay.

JESSIE

What were you going to say?

CHANCE

I was gonna say, it's the one everyone had to read in high school.
> (Beat)
It's happening again.

JESSIE

What? I'm finishing your sentences again?

CHANCE

No, we're connecting again.

JESSIE

Are we?

CHANCE

Aren't we?

JESSIE

I think this is a great idea. I think we should quibble about words.

CHANCE

Me, too. I think if we quibble about words, then—

JESSIE

About the best Thai food, about the worst Thai food, then eventually, you'll wake up from the fantasy land you live in and see that when men and wom—when you and I get together, it eventually ends up in quibbling.

CHANCE

But I don't necessarily see quibbling as bad.

JESSIE

You're saying quibbling is good?

CHANCE

I'm saying quibbling is quibbling. But I think you're afraid of quibbling. I think you're afraid of things being messy.

JESSIE

Why do you say that?

> Chance goes to the other chair and grabs her tote
> from beneath the table. He lifts the tote up onto
> the table and opens it.

CHANCE

(demonstrates and leaves the items out on the table as he talks)

Right pocket zips. When unzipped, we have two tampons for emergency. Left pocket, two identical packs of gum, held together with this clip. Right side compartment. Here we have a checkbook, tidy, with a paper clip to hold the last page. Left compartment, makeup items in small zippable bag. This is what I mean by not being messy. No one's bag is this organized.

JESSIE

I bet Oprah's tote is that organized.

CHANCE

I bet not. Messy is good. Quibbling is good.

JESSIE

I can't tell if you're making fun or you're serious.

CHANCE

I'm sitting in this room with you. And you are this amazing, smart, hot girl.

JESSIE

Don't say that.

CHANCE

And I'm thinkin', if we did this once before, why can't we do this now?

> Jessie finishes her drink, throws the cup on the floor, and gets up from the bed. In her speech below, she quickly puts on her shoes. Then, she starts slamming items into her tote—Chance may try to stop her, but he knows better, as she pulls items out of his hands and the like.

JESSIE

You're fuckin' nuts. I told you, you had this agenda. And I just can't believe you're that stupid. I mean, don't you get it? I left you before, I'll do it again. I don't have the power to stay when things get messy or ugly. It's a life lesson my mother and father both taught me. You don't want to get involved with me because I'm a mess.

CHANCE

You're not a mess.

JESSIE

This can only end badly for you.

CHANCE

You need a friend, Jess.

JESSIE

I've got plenty of friends.

CHANCE

Then you have one more.

JESSIE

I can't be like you, Chance.

CHANCE

Why not?

JESSIE

I'm damaged. Real damaged.

CHANCE

You were.

JESSIE

I still am.

> *Chance gets up from the table and touches her arm.*

CHANCE

Look at me. You're not going back to your dad's shithole. I know it's hard, but you shouldn't see him again.

JESSIE

You talk about being Ozark, but you don't know shit about it. He's blood.

CHANCE

He ain't your blood, Jessie.

JESSIE

But you know he is.

CHANCE

Sometimes, there are lost causes in life. Blood or no blood.

JESSIE

But he's my dad.

CHANCE

He stopped being your father a long time ago.

JESSIE

What about all your *Star Wars* bull shit? What about Luke and Darth Vader, there, Obi-Wan? Luke never gave up on his father.

CHANCE

You're not gonna change him, and he's just gonna use ya till there's nothing left.

JESSIE

So I just give up on him?

CHANCE

By not helping you're helping.

JESSIE

You're so full of shit. You always did like to tell me how to run my life. And you know, I always hated that.

CHANCE

I never tried to run your life. I was just trying to help you when I thought you needed it.

JESSIE

Maybe I didn't need that kind of help. You can't fucking fix everything.

CHANCE

That's fine, Jesse. Maybe you didn't need my help, but your dad, he is way too old to change.

JESSIE

I don't believe that. And why do you care so much about all this anyway? We haven't seen each other in a long time.

CHANCE

Because I'm afraid that no matter what, your goal is to go through tonight all mixed up and alone.

JESSIE

I've been doing it a long time, and I'm used to it.

CHANCE

Good for you. Sounds like a great way to live.

JESSIE

Why so fuckin' mean to me, Chance?

CHANCE

Cuz I want you to snap out of the trance your father and your mother's got you into.

JESSIE

You act like they run my life.

CHANCE

Don't they? Show me the past you're not living right now. You still think about your mom abandoning you and going back to Oregon, you still make trips to the meth shack your dad's living in, you still drink like a fish. You show me how you're living in the now and not in the past.

JESSIE

Fuck you.

Jessie crosses past Jessie toward the door.

CHANCE

Now we're getting somewhere.

  JESSIE

No, Chance. We're not.

                        Jessie gets very close to the door. Chance races
                        over and beats her to it and just stands there.
                        Jessie assesses the situation.

                                    JESSIE (CONT'D)

If I want out, I get out.

                        Chance nods.

                                        CHANCE

One more friend.
                        (Beat)
Plus, I'm not altogether unpleasant to look at while you're
talking.

                        Jessie leans her back against the wall by the door.

                                        JESSIE

That's the thing. I got no one to talk to about this.

                                        CHANCE

Now you do.

                        Jessie pushes off the wall.

                                        JESSIE

You're an idiot.

                                        CHANCE

Yeah.

                        Jessie puts her tote on the table, and plunks down
                        in the chair closest to the bed. She spins the
                        bourbon bottle with her fingers.

Chance crosses and takes up Jessie's former position in the middle of the bed as he leans against the headboard.

                    JESSIE
Nobody gets it. Not even a professional. And it's just ridiculous to even think about talking about it. Or how to talk about it.

                    CHANCE
Stop thinking so much. So you saw a counselor.

                    JESSIE
I was in therapy once. Here in Kansas City.

                    CHANCE
Was it helpful?

                    JESSIE
It helped to bitch about my problems, but I could tell he'd never been poor. He didn't know how desperate Mom and Dad got. How desperate we all got.

                    CHANCE
But surely he understood on some kinda level.

                    JESSIE
That don't mean shit though, does it? Living in the now is a good story, Chance, but I don't know how to do it.

                    Chance leaps up and shoves her out of the chair, then springs back to the bed. Jessie lies sprawled on the floor. She laughs.

                    JESSIE (CONT'D)
You're nuts.

                    Jessie gets back up and sits again.

CHANCE

So.

JESSIE

So.

CHANCE

Here we are.

JESSIE

Here we are.
          (Beat)
Why do you care so much what happens to me?

CHANCE

I just see so much in you. So many incredible things. You're
smart, you're talented, you're really funny, and you get my
stupid jokes. And I think you're really beautiful.

JESSIE

So you are trying to get me in bed?

CHANCE

No. I didn't mean—

JESSIE

So I'm not beautiful—

CHANCE

No. I mean—

JESSIE

I'm just messin' with ya.

CHANCE

I was just trying to say that you have so much potential in so
many—

JESSIE

I'm single.

CHANCE

Huh?

JESSIE

You know earlier when I said I wasn't single?

CHANCE

Yes.

JESSIE

Well. I'm single now.

CHANCE

You mean, you weren't single before dinner, but now you are single?

JESSIE

No, I mean I was single before dinner, and I'm still single now. Not long ago, I wasn't single.

CHANCE

I'm not even going to ask questions because I'm fairly certain I won't understand.

JESSIE

Good. Not that this means anything.

CHANCE

It means we could make out.

JESSIE

Because that's part of connection?

CHANCE

It's an indelible part of connection. Without the making out, you really think, what are we doing?

JESSIE

How does this work with male friends you're connecting with?

CHANCE

Whatever makes them happy. I put their needs before mine.
    (Beat)
What were we talking about?

JESSIE

Who cares when it's going in such an interesting direction.

CHANCE

It seems like I was making a point about something.

JESSIE

You wanted to know about therapy.

CHANCE

How'd that work out for you?

In the following section, Chance and Jessie flirt subtly.

JESSIE

(joking and implying being in the room with him)
Look where I am. Shitty, can't ya tell?

CHANCE

Perhaps your therapist would be proud.

JESSIE

Former therapist.

CHANCE

Perhaps he'd be proud of you for confronting your demons.

JESSIE

I have demons?

CHANCE

We all have demons.

JESSIE

What do yours look like?

CHANCE

Ugly. And they have a bad sunburn. Yours?

JESSIE

Small. Quiet. But not pretty either. So how do we face them?

CHANCE

I'm still working out those details. But that's really not what I'm thinking about right now.

> *Chance scoots closer to her from the bed. Jessie leans in from the chair. The flirting intensifies in the following section.*

JESSIE

I can only imagine.

CHANCE

Thai tacos. That's what I was thinking about.

JESSIE

Really?

CHANCE

The best of both worlds. Mexican and Thai together. A union of spicy and crunchy. A union of the invariably hot.

Pause

It appears they're about to kiss.

Lights down.

ACT TWO
SCENE ONE

Lights up.

Chance, still on the bed, leans close to Jessie in the chair. Jessie backs away from him.

JESSIE

Sure, I'd eat Thai tacos.

CHANCE

Yeah?

JESSIE

I'll try anything once.

CHANCE

Because life is a short sentence?

JESSIE

Because life is a very short sentence.

CHANCE

That chair is really uncomfortable.

JESSIE

It's not that bad.

CHANCE

It's really really uncomfortable.

Chance fluffs a pillow on the bed for her.

JESSIE

I'm good, really.

CHANCE

Are you?

Chance continues to fluff a pillow for her.

Jessie, a bit reticent, rises and sits next to him on the bed. They face forward. They are somewhat close to each other, but their bodies certainly do not touch.

CHANCE (CONT'D)

Did you know the girl? Who died?

JESSIE

No. But it felt like I did.

CHANCE

Do you believe in an afterlife?

JESSIE

I have enough trouble believing in a now life that's meaningful.

CHANCE

So you gave up the Protestant Church?

JESSIE

About the same time you did.

CHANCE

Where do you think we were before we were born?

JESSIE

In an egg.

CHANCE

I mean before that.

JESSIE

Nowhere. You can't have a human without an egg and a body.

CHANCE

So what will happen to you when you die?

JESSIE

Why are you asking me—

CHANCE

Just humor me. When we die?

JESSIE

I guess we'll be like a puff of smoke, Chance.

CHANCE

A puff of smoke?

JESSIE

You know how in the winter you can see smoke coming out of chimneys?

CHANCE

Sure.

JESSIE

The smoke winds and spins and goes up into the air and disappears. We do the same. Sometimes, I really like knowing I'll be gone.

CHANCE

Why?

JESSIE

I'll never have to shave my legs again.
        (Beat)
Stop looking at me like that.

CHANCE

Like what?

JESSIE

Like I've got the answers or something.

CHANCE

Don't you?

JESSIE

For me.

CHANCE

I don't want your answers for me. I just love hearing how your mind works.

JESSIE

Stop that, too.

CHANCE

Speaking to you?

JESSIE

No. Saying sweet things like that.
(Beat)
I'm not sleeping with you.

CHANCE

That's awfully presumptuous, Jess. You're the one who invited yourself up.

JESSIE

Oh shit. That was me?

Chance nods.

JESSIE (CONT'D)

Figures.

                    JESSIE (CONT'D)
        (Beat)
Don't let me sleep with you.

                    CHANCE
No problem.

                    JESSIE
So. The band's good?

                    CHANCE
The band is good.

                    JESSIE
The album is good?

                    CHANCE
The album is really good. I've got copies in my bag.
Chance rises, as needed, and grabs a CD from his duffle bag.
As he sits back down on the bed, he hands the CD to Jessie.

                    JESSIE
Sweet. But I want a signed copy from everybody.

                    CHANCE
Go ahead and take that one for now. I'll get you a signed
copy.

                    JESSIE
Thank you. I'll put it in the very spacious and well-organized
right sleeve.

                    CHANCE
With the checkbook.

                    JESSIE
With the checkbook, you bastard.

CHANCE

Just trying to help out.

JESSIE

Will you help out and put it on the table for me?

Chance rises and puts the CD on the table, then sits back on bed.

JESSIE (CONT'D)

And the tour is good?

CHANCE

Yeah, you meet the coolest people. And some guys who can really play. But it's definitely about lifestyle compensation.

JESSIE

What do you mean?

CHANCE

Ya live off fuckin' coffee, fast food, and cigarettes. Too many hours in the van. And the worst part is showing up to a gig and the sound guy doesn't know what the hell he's doing, and he doesn't know what the hell he's doing on shitty PAs that don't work.

JESSIE

That sucks.

CHANCE

Or the club gives you two drink tickets. What the fuck am I supposed to do with two drink tickets? But some of the clubs though are awesome. And the fans, digging the music. Makes it worth it. And seeing the country's hard to beat.

JESSIE

I bet.

CHANCE

If I'm not sleeping with Rob's elbow in my face, I'll really take in the countryside. Last year, we played in Wyoming. Ya know, when I was a kid, we went there once. I remember the big sky and the bizarre scenery. All that openness, and the spiny sage and how it smelled, and mom and pop motels with neon signs. And I couldn't wait for the motel and the pool and the mini-golf. I remember feeling weightless. How do we lose that feeling?

JESSIE

It's called growing up, I guess.

CHANCE

I guess. Don't know that I really lost it. Did you feel weightless with me?
            (Beat)
We were really good together.

JESSIE

We drove each other crazy.

CHANCE

In a good way. We should start seeing each other again.

JESSIE

Are you nuts?

            Jessie rises and crosses toward the art on the wall
            (the beach scene).

JESSIE (CONT'D)

Just because we're having a nice moment here, doesn't mean we should start that again. And plus, you live—where do you live?

CHANCE

Kansas City.

                    JESSIE
You don't.

                    CHANCE
I do.

                    JESSIE
You live out of a van.

                    CHANCE
I did.

                    JESSIE
Now?

                    CHANCE
Kansas City.

                    JESSIE
You don't.

                    CHANCE
I will.

                    JESSIE
When?

                    CHANCE
At the end of the summer.

                    JESSIE
At the end of August?

                    CHANCE
September.

                    JESSIE
So that's really October.

CHANCE

Let's not quibble on the details.

JESSIE

Why would you choose to live here instead of the Ozarks?

CHANCE

The band.

JESSIE

Don't you miss being at home?

CHANCE

Of course, but right now, we're on the road all the time.

JESSIE

Why should we start seeing each other, whatever that means, then take like a three-month hiatus?

> Chance scoots across the bed toward her and sits on its edge.

CHANCE

It's more like two and a half months. And it's no hiatus. I'm here this weekend. I'll be back in a month. We have a week off in the middle of August. You're the one who's always said space was good for people.

JESSIE

That's a lot of space, Chance.

CHANCE

Depends on your point of view.

JESSIE

From my point of view.

                    CHANCE
That's not the reason.

                    JESSIE
Not the reason for what?

                    CHANCE
Why you don't want to see me.

                    JESSIE
What is the reason?

                    CHANCE
Because you're scared.

                    JESSIE
I'm scared?

                    CHANCE
Probably more like petrified.

                    JESSIE
You don't even want to know.

                    CHANCE
I do want to know.

            Frustrated, Jessie crosses to an area, center stage.
            Chance scoots on the bed, so he still is on the edge
            but facing her, so they can talk.

                    JESSIE
You say you want to know, guys always say they want to
know, but they don't. They don't know what to do with an
emotional girl on their hands.

                    CHANCE
I do.

                                JESSIE

Bull shit.

                                CHANCE

Bull shit.

                                JESSIE

You think I'm easy? That this little chat about my past, my dad,
some psychology speak, and I'm gonna end up being this
angel, this girlfriend—

                                CHANCE

That's not what—

                                JESSIE

You think I'm going to fit into this cute little girlfriend box,
well, I won't. I can't. Yeah, you're right. I'm scared. And you
don't know the half of it. I am fuckin' petrified of letting
someone in, totally fuckin' scared to let someone inside. I may
look pretty and all to you in this little dress, but there's a pane
of glass that stands in front of you. And it's bullet proof. I'm
not sure a fuckin' Uzi would do you any good.

                Jessie crosses to the table.

                                CHANCE

What are you doing?

                                JESSIE

What the fuck does it look like I'm doing?

                Jessie grabs her tote and slings the CD into it.

                                CHANCE

You're not doing that.

                                JESSIE

What? You gonna hold me hostage.

58

CHANCE

No. You do that already.

JESSIE

I'm not a saint, Chance.

Chance rises and crosses slowly in her direction.

CHANCE

I know.

JESSIE

I'm not this amazing, glamorous girl who—

CHANCE

Yes, you are.

JESSIE

I'm not as wonderful as you think I am.

CHANCE

Yes, you are.

JESSIE

You're such an idiot. Aren't you listening now? And besides, the last time we were together, I withdrew from you and went into my own little world, and I was distant from you and impossible to—

CHANCE

I didn't own you. I couldn't and wouldn't make you do anything except what you felt you had to do. No matter how much it hurt me.

JESSIE

So why even have these conversations? Why even tempt fate again? Why be here?

CHANCE

I like my sentence, Jess. It's a good sentence. I love being in the band. I love playing my guitar. I meet women, and some of them are okay. But they don't dazzle me. I just want to be in the same room with you as much as possible. That's all I'm saying.

JESSIE

You don't know what you're saying.

CHANCE

Sure, I do. But if you don't get that—
                    (struggling)
If you don't' get that, then go.

JESSIE

Good seeing you.

CHANCE

You, too.

> Jessie leaves.

> A glum Chance sits down on the edge of the bed.

> A few moments later, a knock on the door. Chance rises and opens the door. Jessie blasts past him and sits on the edge of the bed.

JESSIE

What did you mean that I hold myself hostage?

CHANCE

You drank too much, Jess.

JESSIE

We both drank a lot.

Chance crosses and sits down on the bed.

CHANCE

No. You drank a lot.

JESSIE

But you drank with me.

CHANCE

For about ten minutes.

JESSIE

I wasn't always like that.

CHANCE

And those times I enjoyed very much.

JESSIE

I've got a lot going against me.

CHANCE

We all do.

JESSIE

No, I mean about—

CHANCE

I know. Your father's been a meth-head for a decade. Your mother was an alcoholic, and her parents, and her parents, and so on—

JESSIE

It's a disease. It—

CHANCE

It's not a disease. It's unease. And you know it.

JESSIE

You don't know how difficult all of those odds are, Chance.

CHANCE

No, I don't. But I know you can get some help.

JESSIE

I told you I did.

CHANCE

And?

JESSIE

He was cute.

CHANCE

Oh, Jess.

JESSIE

He did help in some ways.

CHANCE

How did he help?

JESSIE

I take days off now. I can drink and not get drunk. Like a normal person.

CHANCE

That's wonderful.

JESSIE

So am I still a hostage, doc?

CHANCE

You tell me.
        (Beat)
You're missing something, Jess.

JESSIE

Oh, god.

CHANCE

I don't mean—

JESSIE

I'm missing love or my soul mate, or you, or God.

CHANCE

None of that shit, Jessie. And you're finishing my sentences again.
(Beat)
Do you know what the Chinese character for human being looks like?

JESSIE

No, I don't, Sensei.

CHANCE

It looks the same as this.

Chance leaves the bed and grabs two coasters from the ice bucket tray.

CHANCE (CONT'D)
(demonstrates as he talks)
If you take two sticks

JESSIE

Those aren't sticks.

CHANCE

If you take two sticks and lean them up against each other . . . like this . . . then what?

JESSIE

They stand up and don't fall over.

CHANCE

Exactly. Just like us. We lie to ourselves and think that we're all separate beings. But we're all joined together.

Chance sits back down on the bed.

JESSIE

Since when did you become the Dali Lama?

CHANCE

You can joke all you want, Jessie, but you know I'm right.

JESSIE

Can you pull some crystals out of that bag, too?

CHANCE

I don't have to talk to you.

JESSIE

I'm sorry, really. Okay.
          (Beat)
It's just easier my way.

CHANCE

Is it?

JESSIE

I'm happy.

CHANCE

Are you?

JESSIE

As happy as a girl can wish to be.

CHANCE

And how happy is that?

JESSIE

I get up every morning, and Desdemona's there. I have my coffee, we go for a walk. I come back, get dressed, go to work. I have my acting, which is wonderful. Play rehearsal some of my evenings.

CHANCE

And if you don't have play rehearsal, what do you do?

JESSIE

Take Dezzy to the dog park. Sometimes go out with Suze. Watch *Dexter*, read about Amelia Earhart. Eat cake in bed. It's good.

CHANCE

That's a pretty good sentence, Jess.

JESSIE

Yes, it is.

CHANCE

Jesus. How many people's sentences look just like yours? Then, a year from now, they're dead. End stop. Period. Blip. Done. Is that how you want it to go?

JESSIE

Why are you judging me?

CHANCE

Can't we ask for more?

JESSIE

It's easy this way. I don't have to deal with men, with you.

CHANCE

Am I that awful?
        (Beat)

CHANCE (CONT'D)

When was the last time you lost yourself. I mean lost, as in got yourself lost in really good sex. And like, you didn't know if you were going to make it? Like the earth was gonna collapse or somethin'. Cuz you were in love. And long gone. When was that, Jessie? Where is that in this perfect day of yours? Cuz you can say our romance was days on end, whatever the hell that means, but what you just told me sounds like days on end with no love in sight.

JESSIE

You've got such a fuckin' attitude. You're such a glorified saint.

CHANCE

Why? Just because I don't want to be a hermit all my life?

JESSIE

Being alone is good.

CHANCE

Don't you think I know that, believe in that, want that for you?

JESSIE

Do you? You talk a good game. But when I left for two weeks to go to San Diego and see the beach, you weren't too pleased. All I wanted to do was get away with some girlfriends and feel carefree. I wanted to see how grand the ocean was. It was gonna be my first time. I opened up my heart to you. But you acted like you didn't want me to go. And when I got back, you were still pissed.

CHANCE

I know. You are so right. I was such an asshole.

JESSIE

Yeah, you were.

66

CHANCE

I apologize.
>(Beat.)
I was a real jerk.

JESSIE

Yeah, a real jerk.

CHANCE

I'm very sorry. I've always regretted it.

>Pause.

JESSIE

I had been hoping to savor this more. And at least a little bit longer.

CHANCE

And that time at Thanksgiving when I criticized your brother, and we all got into it. I never said sorry for that. I'm sorry.

JESSIE

Thank you.

CHANCE

Despite all my Eastern philosophical notions, I can sometimes be . . . strong-willed and pushy. I know that about me.

JESSIE

Holidays can be hard. Impossible with my family.

CHANCE

Live and learn, right? Maybe we're both growing up.

JESSIE

I don't like the sound of that.

CHANCE

Me neither.

JESSIE

But you're not getting off the hook so easy, Obi-Wan. Are you going to sit there and tell me that having people—no— having lovers in your life is easy?

CHANCE

Yes.

JESSIE

You're so full of shit. You have no fucking grip on reality.

CHANCE

Oh yeah. How's that?

JESSIE

When was the last time you were in a relationship?

CHANCE

We're talking about you.

JESSIE

When?

CHANCE

Six months ago.

JESSIE

Bull shit. Who?

CHANCE

Girl from Seattle.

JESSIE

Fuckin' Seattle?

CHANCE

Fuckin' Seattle.

JESSIE

How did that work out?

CHANCE

There were wonderful things about our time together.

JESSIE

You're going to paint it how you like it.

CHANCE

No. I'm going to live it how I like it. Some relationships are meant to be shorter than others. You just make everything so fuckin' hard.

JESSIE

Really?

CHANCE

Having lovers in your life is hard, but it doesn't have to be impossible. I understand that it might feel better to do what you do and withdraw and be alone, but since when does that make it the best path in life?

JESSIE

Since it makes me happy.

CHANCE

Really? All right, there you go. You're right. What are we talking about then? What am I trying to convince you of? I should just shut the hell up.

Pause.

JESSIE

But I'm enjoying this.

CHANCE
Because I'm getting all worked up?

JESSIE
I don't remember seeing that a lot. You were always steady as
she goes.
(Beat)
You're getting worked up because it's me?

CHANCE
Because I care what the hell happens to you.

Chance sits down on the edge of the bed. Jessie
crosses and joins him.

JESSIE
I wouldn't know how to start. How to be open.

CHANCE
I'm not sure it's something you can consciously decide.

JESSIE
The problem is people always want something from you.

CHANCE
I don't.

JESSIE
But you just said—

CHANCE
What I said was that I cared what happens to you. That means
my agenda for you is your agenda for you.

JESSIE
People don't love the way you're talking about.

CHANCE
You and I have the chance to.

JESSIE
But if I do nothing? Don't reciprocate.

CHANCE
It's too late.

JESSIE
It's too late?

CHANCE
Too late for me. I already love you. So all you have to do is the hardest thing in the world for you.

JESSIE
Which is what?

CHANCE
Receive.

Pause.

JESSIE
You said you had no agenda, and you said I couldn't make a conscious decision to be open.

CHANCE
You and I are talking through this. You may have to wing it.

JESSIE
You're talking shit.

CHANCE
All right, then. Fuck that. Let's stop talking.

                    JESSIE

What?

                    CHANCE

Let's stop talking.

                    JESSIE

Sure.

          They sit in uncomfortable silence.

          Jessie gets up and goes to the table. She grabs a
          plastic cup and the bourbon bottle and tips the
          bottle in Chance's direction.

                    CHANCE

That's not what I had in mind.

                    JESSIE

Me taking my clothes off instead?

                    CHANCE

It might help.

                    JESSIE

I thought we weren't talking.

          This is a crucial moment for Jessie as she
          contemplates having a drink but chooses against.

          Long silence.

          Jessie remains standing at the table.

                JESSIE (CONT'D)

Aren't you afraid I'll stop seeing you again?

                    CHANCE
I've got no room for fear.

                    JESSIE
But you should.

                    CHANCE
It's not my style.

                    JESSIE
Your call two weeks ago made me call off my engagement.

          Silence.

               JESSIE (CONT'D)
One phone call made me drop the love of my life.

          Chance is visibly shaken.

               JESSIE (CONT'D)
Want me now, big boy?

                    CHANCE
Because it was me?

                    JESSIE
Because it was a way out.

                    CHANCE
Did you have the dress?

                    JESSIE
No.

                    CHANCE
Did you have bridesmaids?

                              JESSIE
Didn't want them.

                              CHANCE
Justice of the peace?

                              JESSIE
No, he wanted an event.

                              CHANCE
Did you have a wedding planner?

                              JESSIE
He hadn't gotten that far yet.

                              CHANCE
Why were you engaged?

                              JESSIE
Why did you leave Seattle Slew?

                              CHANCE
Seattle left me. She didn't like my jokes. Why were you
engaged?

                              JESSIE
Security.

                              CHANCE
What kind?

                              JESSIE
All kinds.

                              CHANCE
Makes sense.

JESSIE

Does it?

CHANCE

Makes sense you didn't love him. How's he taking it?

JESSIE

Better than can be expected. I don't think he loved me either.

CHANCE

Then why?

JESSIE

Security.

CHANCE

Maybe you won't need a long grieving period.

JESSIE

Maybe not.

CHANCE

Will you need a rebound man?

JESSIE

Who doesn't?

CHANCE

Perhaps you can forgo one this time.

JESSIE

Why?

CHANCE

You know why.

JESSIE

Even after this.

                    CHANCE
Even after this.

                    JESSIE
Why?

                    CHANCE
It is an eternal mystery why the heart does what it does.

                    JESSIE
Many cardiologists would beg to differ.

                    CHANCE
This could be a good summer for your heart, for mine.

                    JESSIE
But if we did this crazy thing and started seeing each other
and endured this summer hiatus—

                    CHANCE
Two months till I'm living here. At most, two weeks between
visits. That's not a hiatus. That's enjoying time apart.

                    JESSIE
Seriously?

                    CHANCE
All right. Well—

                    JESSIE
Even if we started spending time together, I could just stop.

                    CHANCE
Of course. You could get a phone call.

                    JESSIE
And that doesn't bother you?

CHANCE

I'm not going to govern my actions by fear, or grabbing onto a sense of security that doesn't exist.

JESSIE

But I don't want to be attached at the hip.

CHANCE

I don't see our time together as a jail term or like an assignment. When I'm with you, I'm with you. When we're apart, we're apart. Time in a room with you. That's all I'm asking.

JESSIE

That's it?

CHANCE

That's it.

JESSIE

On the surface, that doesn't look like a lot.

CHANCE

That's because it's not.

JESSIE

Theories always look really good, but reality is a different story.

CHANCE

We often grow into our theories.

JESSIE

And sometimes we lie to ourselves. Take the black holes, for instance. Pure science fiction. But because we want to believe in them, then people do.

CHANCE
Black holes don't exist?

JESSIE
No. People think they are real, but they aren't.

CHANCE
Since when did you become an astronomy expert?

JESSIE
Car trouble.

CHANCE
Huh?

> Jessie crosses to the bed and sits down on the
> other side of Chance.

JESSIE
Last year, I spent a lot of time at the mechanics'. They
subscribe to science magazines. The consensus among
physicists is that black holes do not exist. *New Scientist
Magazine.*
    (Beat)
You might think you're not asking a lot, but you probably are.
You might think there are black holes out there, but there
aren't.

CHANCE
I don't think you know what I'm asking.

JESSIE
I think I do.

CHANCE
How?

JESSIE
Because that's how things work.

CHANCE
What things work?

JESSIE
Jesus, Chance. Don't play dumb. This is how things work
when you start seeing somebody. It starts off with a casual
date or two. Then, there are all these steps before someone
wants to have sex, and then there are all these expectations
not only about that, but about time. And how many times a
day can he text you, or not text you. When does he call, when
does he not call. How long till he drives you crazy with this
habit or that habit. This is how things work with a guy.

CHANCE
Unbelievable. How can you talk in these abstractions? Why
can't you talk about me? The guy right in front of you.

JESSIE
Well, it's just. I don't—

CHANCE
(not angry, more at resigned)
Maybe you're right. If that's how you feel, if time in a room
with you is asking too much, if life is just this great big black
hole illusion, if things are always going to be this dark and
depressive way with you, then I was wrong about you.

Chance gets up and heads to the door.

JESSIE
Where are you going?

CHANCE
I'm done here. I'm going home.

JESSIE

Home?

CHANCE

I live out of a van, remember?

Chance opens the door and exits.

Jessie is stunned.

JESSIE
(to herself)

Oh, fuck it.

Jessie rises from the bed and crosses to the table and her tote. She retrieves her cell phone.

JESSIE (CONT'D)

So out of touch with reality. What does he think this is? Fantasy relationship camp.

Jessie punches her friend's number.

JESSIE (CONT'D)

Hey, Suz.
(Beat)
What are you doing?
(Beat)
My evening's done here.
(Beat)
Oh, Chance can be a real jack-ass. Let's go for beers.
(Pause.)
Of course, I want to hear about your aunt chain-smoking outside the church during Sunday's potluck.

Lights down.

ACT TWO
SCENE TWO

Lights up.

Outside the motel. The sounds of crickets and night insects. The stage is fairly dark, and stars can be cast on the theater ceiling.

Chance sits in a folding lawn chair. Jessie enters but does not see him.

Jessie knocks on the door of a van (imagined).

CHANCE

I'm here.

Jessie is startled, then turns to see him.

JESSIE

Jesus. You scared me.

Chance gets up.

CHANCE

Sorry. Take my seat.

JESSIE

No, I just wanted to say—

CHANCE

I'll get another chair from the van.

Chance exits. The sound of a sliding van door. Jessie remains standing. Chance enters with another folding lawn chair and a small blanket. He throws the blanket to her, and she catches it.

JESSIE

Thanks. But I just didn't want to leave with things on that note.

CHANCE

Have a seat.

Chance unfolds the lawn chair he retrieved and sits in it. Jessie, a bit reticent, finally sits down in the other chair. She covers up with the blanket. Chance looks up into the sky.

CHANCE (CONT'D)

We can sit here and look into the sky where there are no black holes.

JESSIE

I can't believe how well you can see the stars out here.

CHANCE

That wooded area back there helps.

JESSIE

Chance, you just have to understand that I hold myself back. I keep my physical distance from people. And it allows me to keep other kinds of distances, too.

CHANCE

I know.

JESSIE

You're one of the few people—I'm not even talking lovers, here, I'm talking about just people—you were one of the few that I let in to my space. In all ways.

CHANCE

I was very thankful for that. I know you haven't had it easy.

JESSIE

You know how I grew up. Being chased by more than one of my dad's sleazy friends or mom wielding that aluminum bat or oversized broom because of course I was asking for it, and you start to think this is normal, and how do I hide out?, and school is a reprieve. And acting is a great way to be all these people that you'll never be at home. You learn your lines in your bedroom. You walk the floors. The other characters in the play come alive. A kind father, a supportive mother. Or even a deranged boyfriend, sure, or, better yet, summer love in Danny Zuko.

CHANCE

I didn't know you were in *Grease.*

JESSIE

Twice. One of the dancers in the dance contest the first time.

CHANCE

And Rizzo the second?

JESSIE

Can't picture me as Sandra Dee?

CHANCE

Given you used to sneak out of your trailer for motorbike rides in junior high . . . hmmm . . . don't know why I would guess Rizzo.

JESSIE

I was Sandra Dee, just so you know. I got to be the beautiful girl for once.
        (Beat)
Enough. I should go. I told Suze I'd meet her for beers.

Jessie stands up.

                              CHANCE
Do you see that planet on the horizon?

                              JESSIE
Venus?

                    Jessie sits back down.

                              CHANCE
Did you know that Venus passes between us and the sun only
once every 125 years?

                              JESSIE
Since when did you become an astronomy expert?

                              CHANCE
Car trouble.

                              JESSIE
C'mon.

                              CHANCE
Seriously. Van trouble. We broke down in Milwaukee last
summer. We had to stay at this divey motel, and the only
thing on cable worth watching was the Science Channel.

                              JESSIE
So is Venus going to pass between us and the sun tonight?

                              CHANCE
No. It's very rare. But it actually happens twice in our lifetime.

                              JESSIE
Really?

CHANCE

It happed in 2004, and it happens again in 2012. The transit of Venus is important to us because it allows us to understand where we are in the universe.

JESSIE

Which is where?

CHANCE

Right here, right now. So the transit of Venus actually happens in pairs, about eight years apart. Which makes it like the blue whale.

JESSIE

How's that?

CHANCE

Did you know that mammals with the largest hearts always travel in pairs?

JESSIE

I didn't.

CHANCE

And the blue whale has the largest heart in the world. It's as big as my motel room. When blue whales call their mates, it can be heard for miles underwater. That's how powerful their hearts are.

JESSIE

I need to go.

Jessie rises. Then, so does Chance.

CHANCE

Where are you going?

JESSIE

I'm going to meet Susan at—

CHANCE

That's not what I meant.

JESSIE

(lying)

All this poetry doesn't mean much to me.

CHANCE

It's not poetry, Jess. It's not bullshit to make you feel better.
It's what is.

(Beat)

Give me the hypothetical.

JESSIE

Huh?

CHANCE

How your night's gonna be?

JESSIE

Suze will meet me down at Twin City Tavern. We'll have beers,
smoke too many cigarettes. I'll hear the latest adventure of
her aunt. I'll talk about you. She'll agree and be a voice of
reason. We'll stay till last call, then leave shortly thereafter
because we hate officially closing down bars at our age. And
there's the fact I have to go in to work tomorrow. I'll go
home, hug Dezzy, drink two glasses of water, and sleep like a
baby until my alarm goes off tomorrow morning. That's how
it will go.

CHANCE

Sounds like a good night.

JESSIE

Good night, Chance.

Jessie touches his arm and gives him a quick hug.

JESSIE (CONT'D)

Good seeing you.

CHANCE

You, too.

Jessie begins to exit.

JESSIE

And what will you do?

CHANCE

I don't do hypotheticals.

JESSIE

Right.

Jessie's phone rings. She looks at it. Her face is surprised, then concerned.

Jessie answers the phone.

JESSIE (CONT'D)

Hi, Gramma.
        (Beat)
Are you sure Dad didn't—
        (Pause)
Okay.
        (Beat)
I will.
        (Beat)
Bye.

CHANCE

What's going on?

                    JESSIE
My dad's in ICU.

                    CHANCE
Oh, Jessie.

        Chance crosses to her, and they hug.

        *Jessie's phone rings. She pulls away from Chance,
        takes two steps away, and looks at her phone.*

                    JESSIE
It's Susan. I don't think I can—

        The phone rings out until it stops.

        *Jessie contemplates leaving, but she can't because
        she allows herself to feel for Chance.*

        *She's scared, but she moves toward Chance. They
        stand close to each other.*

                JESSIE (CONT'D)
Why do they travel in pairs?

                    CHANCE
What?

                    JESSIE
The blue whales. Why do they travel in pairs?

                    CHANCE
They don't always.

                    JESSIE
But you said, most do.

CHANCE

Most do.

JESSIE

But you don't know why?

CHANCE

It's a mystery. Like Venus showing up where it does every 125 years.

JESSIE

How long will Venus be out tonight?

CHANCE

About another hour.

JESSIE

Is that a long time?

CHANCE

On Venus, time moves faster.

JESSIE

How's that?

CHANCE

Remember that German physicist with the crazy hair?

JESSIE

Time is relative.

CHANCE

Yes.

JESSIE

And the hearts of blue whales?

CHANCE

They change everything around them.

Chance holds out his hand.

CHANCE (CONT'D)

Give me your keys.

Jessie hands Chance her keys.

CHANCE (CONT'D)

I'll drive.

They kiss.

Lights fade out.

CURTAIN